THE PINK PUFF

www.the-pink-puff.de

KAREN ANN TEPPERIS
NÉE LAKE

THE PINK PUFF

poems & sketches
Gedichte & Skizzen

Karen Ann Tepperis "The Pink Puff"
poems & sketches / Gedichte & Skizzen

Umwelthinweis:
Alle bedruckten Materialien dieses Buches sind säure- und chlorfrei.

Bibliografische Information der Deutschen Nationalbibliothek
Die Deutsche Nationalbibliothek verzeichnet diese Publikation in der Deutschen Nationalbibliografie; detaillierte bibliografische Daten sind im Internet über http://dnb.d-nb.de abrufbar.

Bibliographic information published by the Deutsche Nationalbibliothek
The Deutsche Nationalbibliothek lists this publication in the Deutsche Nationalbibliografie; detailed bibliographic data are available in the Internet at http://dnb.d-nb.de.

Erstausgabe – Erste Auflage – *First Edition*
© 2009 Karen Ann Tepperis, Darmstadt
Alle Rechte vorbehalten. *All rights reserved.*

Herausgeber und Satz: Stephen Tepperis
Umschlaggestaltung: Thorsten Hecht, Dipl.-Grafikdesigner, Pfungstadt
Herstellung und Verlag: Books on Demand GmbH, Norderstedt

ISBN-10:   3-8370-8243-1
ISBN-13: 978-3-8370-8243-2   www.the-pink-puff.de

I dedicate this book to my eldest son, Stephen,
for the interest he has shown,
and all the work he has put into getting this book published.

CONTENTS

Vorwort

Lange Zeit im Verborgenen verblieb dieser Rohdiamant – eine Gedichtsammlung entstanden während Schulzeit, Studium und Reisen.

Zum Titel: „The Pink Puff" - gesprochen: [ˈpʌf] - ist ein Pseudonym, welches eine Dozentin von Karen Ann Tepperis in England für sie erfand, als sie völlig in pink gekleidet mit einem dazu passenden bauschigen Oberteil zum Seminar am Rolle College heran gerannt kam. „Here comes the pink puff!" hieß es dann. Auch diese Begebenheit zählt zu den Erinnerungen, die mit den Gedichten dieses Buches einhergehen.

Heute, selbst Lehrerin, würden ihre Schülerinnen und Schüler sie wohl aufgrund Ihres Kleidungsstils eher als „Leoparden-Lady" bezeichnen, oder, mit vorgehaltener Hand, „Shakira" (arab.: „die Anmutige"), weil dies ihr musikalischer Künstlername ist (allerdings, und das betont sie, seit mehr als 15 Jahren).

Die Gedichte handeln von dem Generationenkonflikt, Ängsten, Liebe sowie Jugend und Alter, obwohl Karen selbst zur Zeit der Entstehung der Gedichte erst eine junge Erwachsene zwischen 16 und 20 Jahren war.

Die Originale befinden sich nicht etwa auf einem Speicher-Stick oder einer CD-ROM – sie wurden noch nicht einmal mit einer Schreibmaschine getippt, sondern sie fanden ihre Verwahrung in einem gebundenen Notizbuch, welches Karen damals mit sich führte und stetig mit Ihrem Füller veredelte.
Viele Jahre verschwand dieses inzwischen patinierte Schreibbuch jedoch in den Tiefen der Regale ihres Arbeitszimmers, wohl wissentlich wo es lag.

Und nun, verehrte Leserin und verehrter Leser, halten Sie Ihr persönliches Exemplar dieser lyrischen Werke in gedruckter Form in Händen.
Wir hoffen, es ist für Sie ebenso eine Bereicherung, wie für uns.

Darmstadt, im März 2009   Stephen Tepperis

Preface

My poems deal with the generation gap, with loneliness, youth and old age (although I was only a teenager at the time of writing them), with conformity, fear to show true feelings, the fear of getting older, relationships, and, of course, love.

I say "of course", because so many poems and songs deal with the theme of love. This is perhaps the strongest emotion that we can feel and thus it seems easier, logical even, that we write about it. I think when a feeling is so strong, the writing just pours out of the pen! In fact the words have often to be written down fast, otherwise the word flow will stow and the memory of those overflowing words will be lost forever, even before reaching the paper.

I can on more than one occasion remember sitting up in bed in the night to jot down notes for a poem that came to mind. If I hadn't done so, these thoughts, lines of poetry, would have been gone for ever.

I was somewhere between 16 and 20 years of age when writing these poems. An excellent age to feel emotion intensively, and to write about it!

The poems are divided roughly into four phases: my school time, a school trip on a coach to Switzerland, my student phase in Devon (South England) and a journey to India (also on a coach – one of 20 coaches[1] with other students to India).

The last poem "Tomorrow I will sparkle" first seems to show life's journey going in an optimistic direction. But then, why should I sparkle tomorrow? Why not here and now? What is up? We don't get to know what has happened to have to put the optimistic emphasise only on the future.

---

[1] Journey with 500 university students from England in 20 coaches (ca. 26 students per coach). The project was Comex and it was an exchange programme of art and culture, the main target being New Delhi, India.

The title of my book "The Pink Puff" is based on the name I was given by one of my tutors at Rolle College in Devon. On occasions I came late for classes and the tutor could see me through the window, running over the grass to her class. As I often wore a vermilion pink mini dress and vermilion pink stockings, she nick-named me "the pink puff". With her comment: "Ah, the pink puff is hurrying across the field again," I was branded for the whole of my student life, "the pink puff".

I drew the sketches accompanying many of the poems. Some of them show a girl with long curly flowing hair. I have always had such hair myself – so in some way it is a self-portrait. Today at the age of almost 60 years I had intended to finally cut my long dark hair. But I haven't managed to take this step yet. Perhaps tomorrow!

Karen Ann Tepperis, 2009

She Wears a Robe of Lavender Lace   (1964)

She wears a robe of lavender lace
                     Which covers all except her face
And pretty shoulders lean and bare.
                     By the birch you'll always find her there
At night to weep for her love so dear
                     Who left with another, leaving her fear
And hatred for she who drove him away.
                     She believes he will come back someday.
Begging forgiveness; pleading for love.
                     Bringing her presents, a ring; a dove.
But oh! This lady cruel and fair
                     Will flutter her lashes and comb her hair,
To tease her love who was untrue.
                     But then she'll whisper: "I love you."

To Robbie   (1966)

Scruffy should have been his name.
Hairy, scarey,
Funny lad.
His flabby jaws,
Great soft paws,
And other things
That dogs do have.

His curly hair
Quite long and fair,
And oh so scraggy grown!
His jollity,
Popularity,
And enormous appetite.

He frolics free
And lazily.
He yawns and fights
Dramatically.
He plays with children
Lovingly,
And whines for walks
In woods.

A wholesome, carefree
Cheeky boy.
With such a zest
For living.
He can bark and wail,
His curly tail
Flying high,
Like waving wheat.

Pampered plenty;
He knows the love
And fuss
That is his
From us.

He is sleeping now,
A bloated beast,
Sprawling legs and ears.
Dotted eyes,
Big black nose,
Hideously held
Whilst in repose.
Breathing deeply,
An occasional moan.
He is easily pleased
And fatly grown.
Relaxed,
Contented with a bone.

A Lonely Spot   (1966)

A lonely spot
Dwindling small and modest.
Adumbrating black.

Slowly it moves,
Groping in the dirt
Of all mankind.

Weak at heart,
Ostensibly strong
Before the mass.

Trailing teardrops
In the mud
Composed of nothing.

Tinted with disgust
Regret and longing.
Painted with new hope.

So here I sit
Not knowing why
Or how.

Reminiscence

When I do think of Kenwood Grounds
I feel the surge of past contentment pass my mind.
The walk alone, along a leafy lane
When chat of brother Ian,
Certain still to marry that same Moira,
Engages us two both for precious moments long.

Descending spots of people
Speckled in the greenery below, fidget lazily
Beneath those powerful bars of summer heat.

Oh! I am proud to walk beside my love, of days gone by,
When he didst squeeze my fingers, and smile with kindly eyes.
When he didst whisper, soft and low, I would this
Summer day were everyday with you, for such a day
As 'tis, should not be overlooked, or ne'er forgot.

And so we two would wander through the day so short
Like two young things bound in a mutual feeling, rare and sweet.
Clutching each one's hand as on we walk. Alack;
To look back on a time so fair,
Who would have e'er believed that it could end? As did.

Homework

I see the paper-stack of white.
I see the gentle drip of ink.
I see the pile of paper-backs.
I hear the silence cut the night.

I glance at my bed with the yellow coverlet.
I imagine the warmth concealed within.
I imagine the fair dreams ready to drift
Into lands of unknown, where kindness is Queen.
A tempting diversion: she beckons her finger
Like Eve, and I, being Adam, must fall in the trap.
I put down my pen, and walk to my bedside.
Climb slowly up and lay down to rest.
Oblivious to all else, but sweet sleep and comfort,
Where dreams must mature till dawning light.

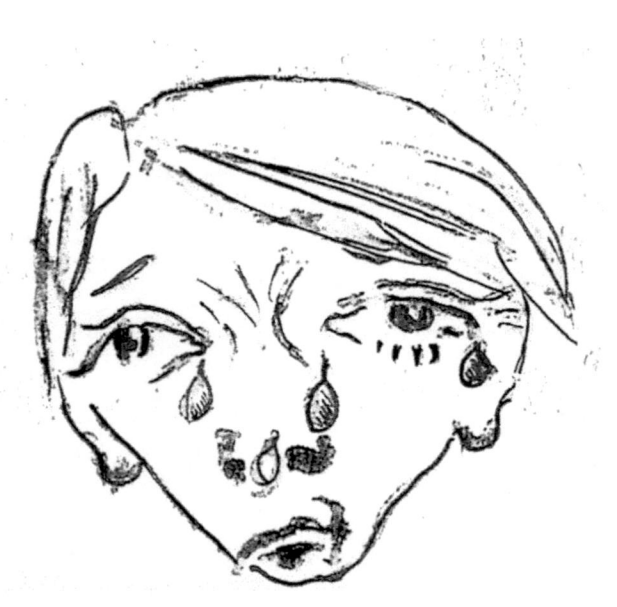

Please Don't Cry! She Said.   (1966)

"Please don't cry!" She said,
When their stomachs rumbled.
"Please don't cry!" She said,
When their hand stretched out.
"I know I am your mother, and I love you just the same,
But I cannot give you what I have not got."
She prayed; they watched; she was good to mankind;
they followed her example.

"Please don't cry!" She said,
To their eyes appealing.
"Please don't cry!" She said,
To their eyes amazed.
"I know you are too hungry, and your bodies are all bone,
But there must be some whose life is even worse."
She sighed; they shivered; she wept; they smiled.
"Please don't cry!" They said,
When she covered her face.
"Please don't cry!" They said,
When her tears flowed freely.

"We know you do your best for us,
We love you just the same,
But we wish we had some more than nought to eat.

Sunset (1966)

Cream and amber, purple pink,
One would not think there could be
Such a splash of colour lurking there.

It is not fair to only see it once a day.
A magnificent array of glowing warmth set in gold
And ivory, old, but physically young and modest light
Glinting bright, before the fall of silent night
Descends; transforming white to sombre shades of darkest grey.
Sweeping away puffs of peach, and blobs of blue,
Out of view and then into a harder, bolder, stronger sphere.
We cannot hear the gloom appear but feel it tread
Upon our head, a creeping creature black.

Love's Elegy   (1966)

I thought I had you in my fist
Hard and fast and easily.
I thought I had you for consumption;
Squeeze the juice, then digestion.
Confidence was all I had;
A mere word where love is concerned:
Please forgive me.

You were taken. She held you firmly
Within that breast.
A female claw, digging deeply. Ever fruitful
In your mind's eye.
Though she remorseless and wilted grown,
You will love her till the end.
She knows you belong to her.

And I, a lonely thing,
Will pine for you.

A Water Sonnet   (1965)

Shining waters rarely seen,
Of brilliant blue, and evergreen.

Wavering o'er the approaching tide,
Carrying crabs, who've come for the ride,

To spare their little legs so sweet
From swimming in the hovering heat.

Oh, fish so fine with fins divine
That sparkle in this land of mine

And yours! If you would like to take
The world as 'tis, for you can make

A pleasure from the sea and air
Which belongs to us, with some to spare.

Be thankful for what has been created;
For this is the way the world was fated.

To That Person Who Made an Affectionate Impression.

He thinks I think I know not what.
A touch, a glance, I cannot tell
From this, or that, how he doth act
Within that frame concealed from me.

He hath a twinkling eye of blue.
But come to think, perhaps 'tis green.
Though I care not for colours tune
When I can have a song from him.

His ways are ways of everyone,
But everyone hath not his ways.
For he doth act what he doth say,
And they do say what they would act.

He hath a virtue soft and sweet
Could crack that shell grown hard and rough.
If he would let it trickle in
And fill the space between the crack.

He hath the power to melt my words
That cut like ice and hurt intently,
And I am left a blunt edged creature
Impotent, like a stingless snake.

If he would show me all the beauty
I have chanced to catch a glimpse of,
I would thank him dutifully,
And proudly kneel before his feet.

Oh don't you know it's you
That clipped the edges of my hatred.
Embraced my folly lovingly,
Destroying my distrust in man.

At dawn of day, a tranquil hour,
I wonder if his thoughts are mine.
He feeds me all I ever crave for;
Life for living; truth for trust.

Sincerely my true mind hath wandered
Pursuing truth and warmth and him
He stands unique and unaffected,
A living soul, among the dead.

Oh Moon.   (1966)

Oh moon, oh moon, I do confess that I have
Fallen wholeheartedly in love with you.
Does it please you so to hear?
A beauty unique and rare as yours is surely often
Gazed upon with wondering eye.
I am enchanted by that silver solitude;
Captivated by that serene smile.
You are bound in the mood of equanimity.

Oh moon, oh moon, a creamy colour, soft and light
Is whisked well before my eyes to a pure substance.
Jacketed in robes of black, such dismal night-wear
Cunningly brings out the best of that beautiful body.

Oh moon, oh moon, whilst lying here, I stare at you
Until my view begins to fall, and I am rather sleepy grown.
I snatch an hour or two of rest, and for a while
Forget your presence, whilst walking hand in hand with pleasant
dreams.
But in the morning I awake and find you gone.

Why desert me so unjustly?
Steal away when mine eyes are closed?
My peace of mind is taken with you;
The following night it will return.

Loneliness   (1966)

Sitting by the grimy window
Too high for her to dust;
Too low to attract much sunlight,
She watches those few souls
Too busy to stop and chat;
Too selfish to smile or wave,
Who pass her way occasionally.

Hoarding memories in her mind
Too ancient for accurate detail;
Too far away for clear remembrance.
She smiles, as though not used to the act
Too gay for one so old;
Too joyous for one without cause.
She lives alone, uncared for.

She has reached her moment
Of dark despair and lifeless living.
She has reached her hour
Of futile existence where nothing matters.
She has used her last tear.
What lies beyond that apathetic stare?

Don't give up!
Don't lose heart and die defeated.
Fight back and win;
Too proud to fall so easily;
Too stubborn to make way for death.

A Little Girl   (1967)

A little girl is something special.
What a pity she cannot realize her speciality until it is too late.
When she is a woman grown.
A little girl yearns to be thrice her age;
But why, oh why? For that day will come soon enough.
Her skin, unflawed by a pink rice-pudding picture
Is petal smooth and soft as peach,
But she does not appreciate that skin.
Instead she craves to paint it gaily,
Hideously even, just like her mum's.
But why, oh why? For that day will come soon enough.
She knows not of worldly worries,
Though observant eyes may sense a grief.
Living in luxury dreams of magic
Where imagination is all she requires,
She has the whole universe at her feet to play with.
If only she knew her true fortune before it is gone.

The Dilemma.   (1967)

Am I mad?
Or is the world mad?
Who can answer
This reasonable question?
For he who says:
"'Tis you who's mad!"
Is conforming with the rest.

Do they ever think
Perhaps they are mad,
And I am sane?

Death.   (1967)

Death is something we all have in common.

It is born, flourishes, and withers.
Filled with morose and adumbrating black,
It looms above the radiant sky, called heaven.
Waiting for a chance to pounce on prey.

Where death treads, life follows.

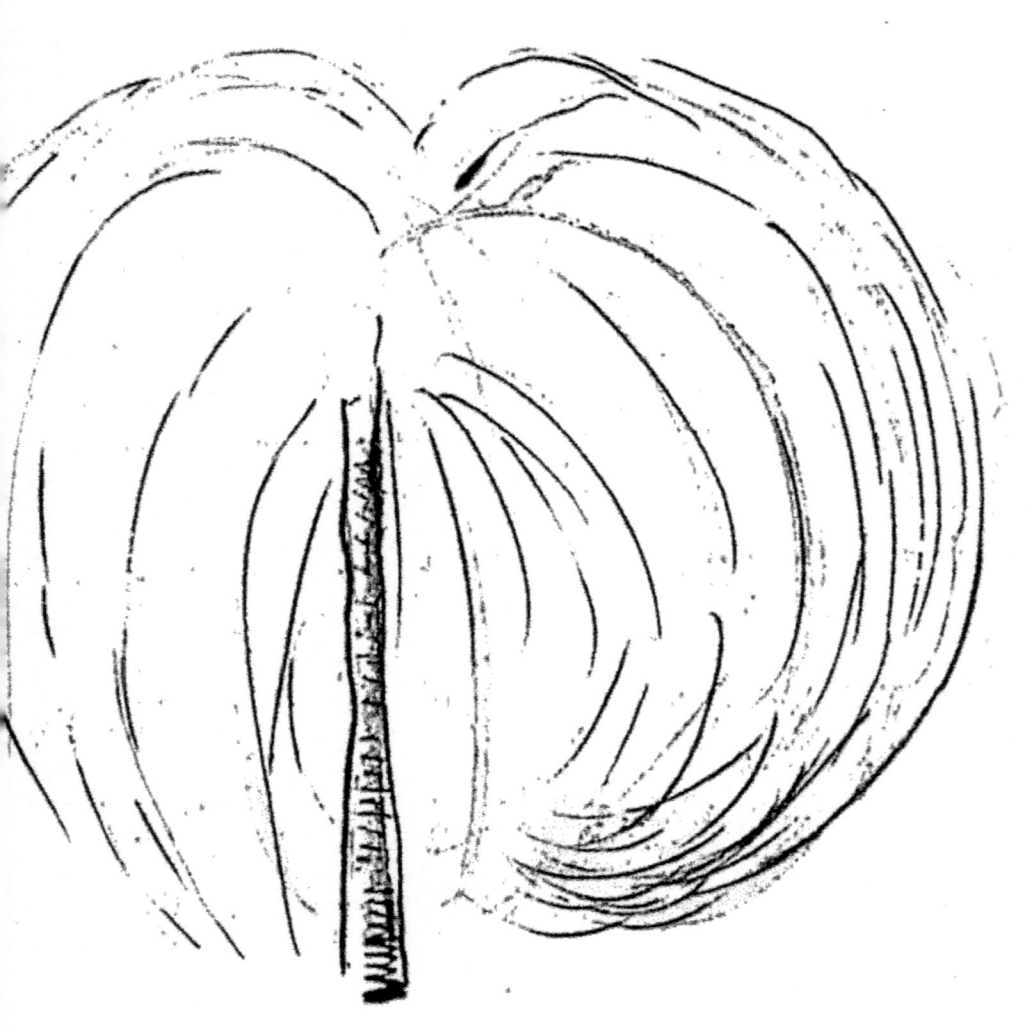

Willow Tree.

Come weeping Willow, cry with me,
You have no one to comfort thee.
Sad and lonely, lovely tree,
I'll comfort you; you comfort me.

We have no friends or neighbours too,
For truer friends, they number few.
Oh, for one to be so true!
You smile for me; I'll smile for you.

Come weeping Willow, lie with me
And watch the fresh grown greenery.
Our world cannot yet sweeter be,
Until we two both wiser be.

Allegory of 5 Fruits.

There is a season in the year
In which the farmer picks the apples.
Proudly lays them in a loft
To ripen daily; and mature.

Too bad he overlooked an apple
Threw it in with all the rest.
Only there to bruise and batter,
Contaminate the crop of fruits.

The farmer feels his duty over,
Smokes his pipe, relaxes easy.
Awaits the arrival of the new batch
Which grow green three seasons long.

Why then does the farmer miss
The apple bruised and ever bruising?
Lets it scatter on the good ground
There to choke and there to throttle.

Like the bad seeds in the Bible:
Thistles crushing baby flowers.
Like the spider capturing prey
Enticed by surface loving network.

Like the trap that's set for mice,
When caught their call is gone unanswered.
They are murdered, done away with,
Who should care about those mice?

(cont'd.)

Like the snares that's set for fowl
Whose fate, determined by appetite,
Whose living soon shall end forever,
Only to exist by name.

And what about that farmer's apples
Left maturing individually?
Does each acquire a colour and flavour
To suit its taste and type of tree?

It is were truly so it would be
Success for every apple tree.
You, I see, are Granny Smith,
Whilst I, the purest Laxton be.

But truth would tell that Laxton's one day
Soon affect a Granny Smith shape.
A Cox's Pippin tasting apple
Really is a Bramley's Seedling.

And when one apple, slightly bruised
Is laid in lofts with flawless fruit,
Time will show the bruise grown larger,
Anchored deep in shallow water.

With each new day – births of bruises,
Until they cluster altogether.
Identical in size and shape.
Identical in taste and colour.

Over ripe, most fruits are taken
From the loft to other quarters,
Shops and houses, other countries,
All to be consumed thereafter.

(cont'd.)

Only five fruits still lay hidden
In that small loft, warm and cosy.
Sheltered from the wintry weather,
Ripening from seeds once callow.

At first the folly lay in one fruit,
Soon enough it doubled number.
Then the couple raised its total
Two – a trio – and quartet?

The apples once quite fresh and juicy
Are the victims of contagion.
Four apples, rotten to the core.
Has the fifth made one more?

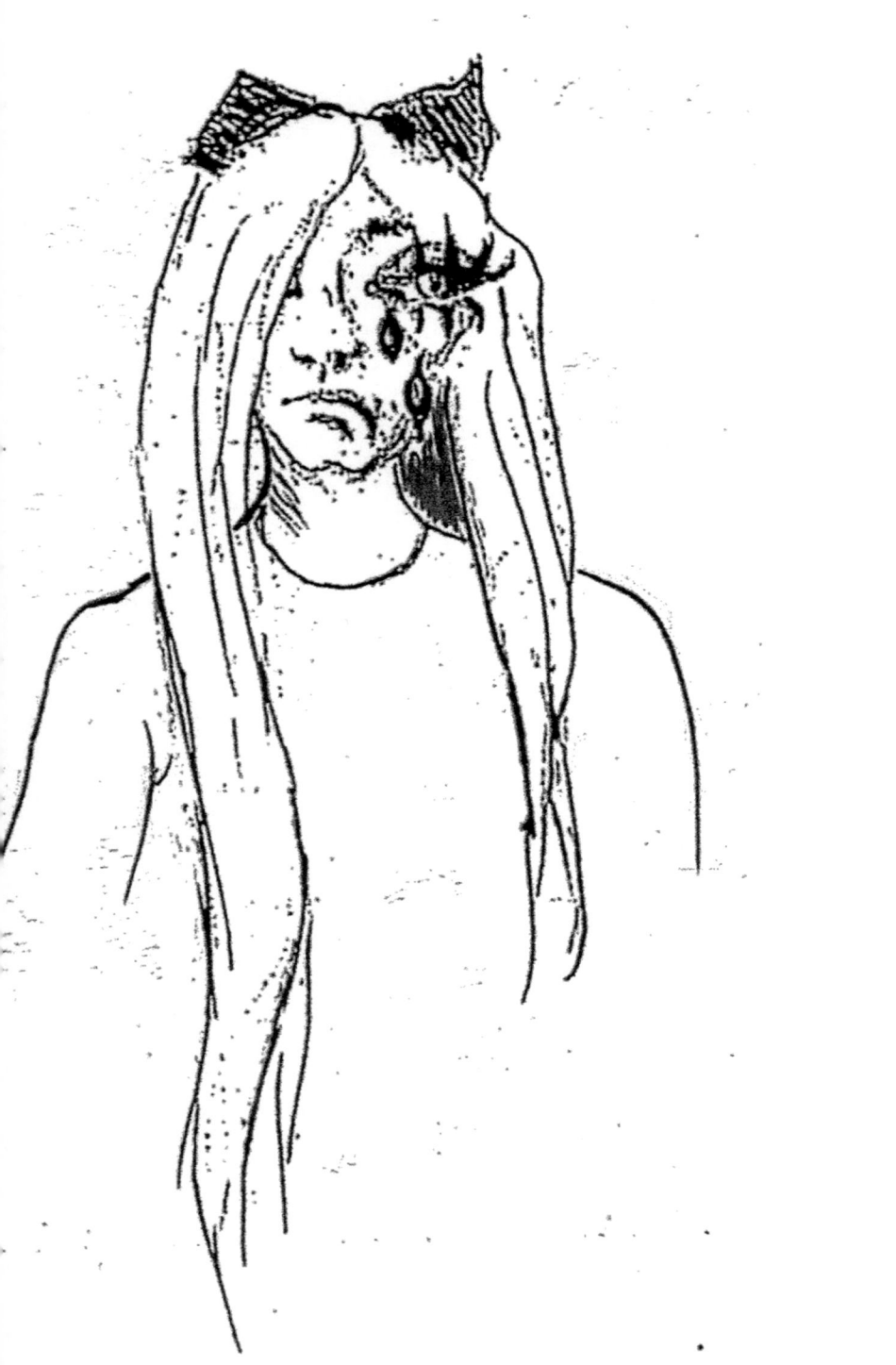

His love has left him on his Own

His love has left him on his own
The way a dog would leave a bone
After having had its fill.

His heart, 'tis broke a thousand parts
— So much for women's human hearts
To taint vile lust and ill led truth.

Oh wicked woman where's your shame!
On you, his sorrow I place blame,
As you, on him, bestowed deceit.

Won't you take him back again
Or am I pleading all in vain?
You are the only one to heal.

Though I am here, don't get me wrong,
My wish is not to see him belong
To you, for now, or ever more.

I should rather see his life
Lived throughout with me, his wife,
My only worldly wish of joy.

I cannot have what is not mine
So I should like to see him thine
If it will make his life complete.

Accept his love and in return
He'll love you more, and I will yearn
My life away for love of him.

Nonsensical Limericks.

There was an old man from Spain
Had legs of Chinese bamboo cane.
"I don't mind at all
If they're skinny and tall,
I use them as oars in the rain."

There was a young woman from Eard
Was thought to be funny and weird.
"I don't care," she said,
"If you laugh till your dead,
When I wear my big black beard."

There was a young man from Exmoth[i],
Was filled with such anger and wroth.
"The taxes I pay
Are squandered away
By those bloody Rolle[ii] students by Goth!"

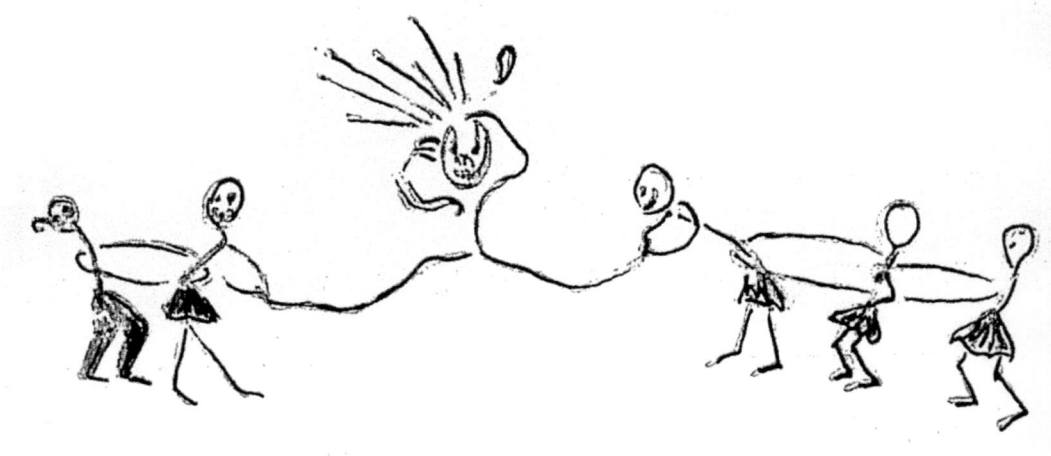

PARANOID.   (1967)

You can hurt me with a stone,
Tear me down and leave alone.
Break my back and wish me dead,
Pulverize my aching head.
Watch the blood seep from my vein,
See me mad, though once quite sane.
Curse and kick my every might
Until it dwindles out of sight.
Derisively attack my wit,
Replacing it by something fit
To strike a blow at me that stings.
But I shall fight with other things
Like courage, confidence and will
Before you over-ride and kill
My ego, and validity.
You will not humiliate me.
Though pains you take to see me sad,
I shall just be twice as glad,
And only linger one short spell
On why you choose to give me hell
Instead of friendship, love and joy:
Pleasure that will never cloy.
What a waste of energy
Spent on ridiculing me.
Though you may think I face defeat,
I never shall by you be beat.

Switzerland.

Part I.

Perhaps I'll think of cable-cars
Dancing precariously on the high wire,
Showing off their talents
To animated dozens.

Perhaps I'll think of Montreaux, Geneva and Lausanne,
Where one is given opportune moment to practice French on friends.

I may just think of snow-time,
When toboggans topple upwards-woe-time!
Inevitably I should be exhausted.
That's when I think of bed-time.

Perhaps I'll think of faces, familiar at school,
So strange to travel with them all.
Get to know the interior of that face.

I may think of Toby, the driver of that coach,
A cheeky wrinkled droopy-eyed cocker-spaniel doggyfied faced friend.
Always has a smile and a kindly word for all of us.

Beauty cannot be ignored
When pondering o'er that region.
For lake and land go hand in hand
To make a picture truly grand.

It's possible I'll linger a while
On French francs, salami, or spinach.
Maybe rich chocolate cakes shaped like mountains
Filled with soft white cream like snow:
I ate loads of snow filled mountains.

Perhaps I'll think of those who hog the chips,
And those who drink till they are merry
So that they find themselves telling others about who
They used to hate before they knew,
But now, perchance, may like.

What of those who after one intimate chat
Can find they don't despise,
But like a little – such surprise!
For those who hate in vain.

Perhaps I'll think of that German barrier
That was knocked for six.
And that cracked wheel which caused us
To miss the last ferry from Calais
But Dunkirk served for us
And ferried us away.
If we had stayed at Calais
We would have lost a day.

Part II.

But more than food and France and fifth-forms
I will think of individuals
Whom I have chanced to meet.
New friendships born of hatred,
Old malice killed from shame.
An apology accepted in a cellar,

Melancholy, confusion, youthfulness.
There is only one way it may lead –
The way of happiness.

I will think of shopping for Chinese cups
And memories of 'weirdies',
Laughter and a pang of pride
Walking in that trio.

I will think of rubber bands and shoe laces,
And maroon necks.
Of snowballs that were pelted,
Of snowballs I returned.

Cast my mind to palm reading
Lonely walks and Emma Peel.
Joan Baez, orange dolls, black boots and cheese.

I will think of dancing,
Of being too proud to approach those I favour,
Slighting those I care for, hurting those I like,
In hope that they will notice
And play my game with me – I wonder if they notice?

I will think of watches, as big as medallions
With gay straps and loud ticks.
A fur coat soft enough
To rest wet eyes upon.

I will remember laughter,
Observance that perceives too many teeth
Too much gum –
A dramatic laugh.

And what of wasted time?
I will think of that.
Time which could have been spent
In other company.

Part III.

The happiest moment I will think about
Was the tenth night – the last.
It was 3 o'clock in the morning
And dark and raining.
I thought the journey over
And that relationship had died –
Even though it was not born.
Then like an answered prayer
The seed of the unborn relationship
Gave birth in an offer to take home
My parents, my suitcase,
And me.

The Journey in a Coach.   **(On the way to Switzerland)**

Miles and miles to travel,
Nothing much to do.
      I've read my book
      Took a look
At scenery in blue.
So now I look at you.

One seat ahead you sit,
So near and yet so far.
      To see you there,
      Hair so fair,
How wonderful you are.
So close but yet too far.

There's one thing I should like
for you to ask of me
      Quite sincere,
      Hear a tear
Trickle down humbly.
"May I sit with thee?"

I do not understand
The glance you pass my way.
      Nice or not
      Cold or what
Wont you ever say
If I should go or stay?

The wheels engulf the road
Evening cannot keep
      From silent night.
      Bright and light
Inside, a muffled weep –
Someone cannot sleep.

Wont you sit beside me?
I should like to know
      Either way,
      Yay or nay,
My feelings I shan't show
Though I like you so.

Love.

I should like a companion —
Chaperon, friend, brother, all knit in one.
A youth whose tongue would not be tied
When talking of a future bride.
He should be able to talk to me
Of the things we hear, and see
And think about, then to discuss
Without embarrassment all that fuss
The male and female seem to find –
What a peculiar state of mind.
When he has me for a date
I wonder why he can't relate
His inner thoughts to me?
He cannot see I'm not looking for a mate,
Just a friendly friend.

When boy meets girl
Why is she coy? For heaven's sake
'Tis only a boy, or youth, or man
That she befriends.

So many people seem to think they find
A perfect frame of mind
For love
Well founded, grounded, suitable
For either one.
At times
Perhaps they are blind.

(cont'd)

I cannot comprehend some situations
Wherein malice, grudge, and jealousy
Cap the bottle of loveless, lifeless liquid
Mistakenly called
Sweet and tender love.
I cannot send messages of sympathy
To those lost souls,
Doomed from the start
To witness heartache, cruelty,
War-fare.
Besides, they do not know they need sympathy.
They have 'no tools for living'.
I should lend a kindly word
To those who cannot see,
But I don't.

Love is not the thing for me,
Such luxury I find impossible.
Why cant I have an honest friend,
A neighbour near me to the end,
Of opposite appeal?
A relationship quite understood
A realationship quite real.

No need for him to be elite,
Or sweet.
No need for him to be acclaimed
Or famed.
He may have one vice, or more
As long as he is nice, I'm sure
He'll suit my fickle needs.

(cont'd)

No need for him to be a beauty
But he must not think it my duty
To uphold that sentiment.
No need for him to be of great physique,

So what if he is thin and weak!
For tales so often tell of books
That never should be judged by looks!
An interesting jacket may not be
Half so much inside.

So what if he is ugly fat?
I say I do not care of that.
The owner of a sharpened wit
Will gladly swell my pride.
A person wise enough
To appreciate the simple joys of life.
If he is lively and sincere
There'll always be a place in here;
My heart.

But no – today this cannot be,
Love is not the thing for me,
And neither is a friendship dear,
For I fear, I ask too much
From hearts too small.
They cannot give me all –
Or will not.

In time to come,
I will find a mind
To match my own.
But as to yet;
Fruit, it will not bear I know,
Only hurt, and sad-sorrow.

The Image.

Shadowing along the walk
Tall and dark and large:
Yet not so large
As to forget
All kindliness.

               Slinking along the isle
               Calm and confident:
               Yet not so confident
               As to forget
               Some days of doubt.

Stepping along the corridor
Aging and mature:
Yet not so mature
As to forget
All youthful love.

               Moving along the way
               Shy and fit and strong:
               Yet not so strong
               As to forget
               All gentleness.

Walking along the hall
Quiet and unassuming
Yet not so unassuming
As to assume
Respect is won.

(cont'd)

Edging along the side
Dignified and proud:
Yet not so proud
As to forget
All humbleness.

The Death of Life.   (1967)

What has happened to emotion
Given out in deep devotion:
Love from friendship; strength from pain,
Cant we bring it back again?

Humanity has long been dead –
Crumbled like a broken straw.
The death of life it has been said
Will linger on forever more.

No bright blood colours ruby red
Drop down on us like falling rain.
No cheerful tunes inside the head
Flowing with a glad refrain.

The only colour near to red
Is danger, lurking overhead,
Screaming bodies under fed,
And bloody bodies of the dead.
Bloody bodies of the dead.

The only tune inside the head –
A funeral march, result from war.
The song of life it has been said
Is dead and gone for evermore.
Dead and gone for evermore.

Love from friendship, strength from pain
Is too melodious a refrain.
Lamenting thus is all in vain
For black is brown and black again.

Inferiority Complex.   (1967)

Sit down a while and talk to me
Of all the things that bother you
Although of late you act so shy
And blush bright red
And stutter a little
And stumble for words
Confused in thought
Initiative lacking
Pathetic fool
I'll talk to you in softly tones
You will not have to dive for cover
Conceal your blush
And be so shy

I'll tell you just where you went wrong
And you will say
"If I had known, if I had known."
There'd be no need to carry on
This futile play – this tragedy
This ever living lifelessly

And you will stage your long lament
And you will bow your head and cry
Go on, go ahead and weep a while
Drench those eyes in silky tear-lets
Soak that face and neck in pearl drops
Then laugh aloud
Release yourself from basic emotions

Why are you always conscious of your role
To tread lightly?

(cont'd)

Conscious of your complex, inferiority,
Guilt, ignorance, apatheticness,
Unadventuresome spirit
Believe me
It is all in the mind
A way to escape

But you can tell me what you wish I will try to understand
Though subjectiveness may mingle with
Innocence and ignorance
For I know you so well.

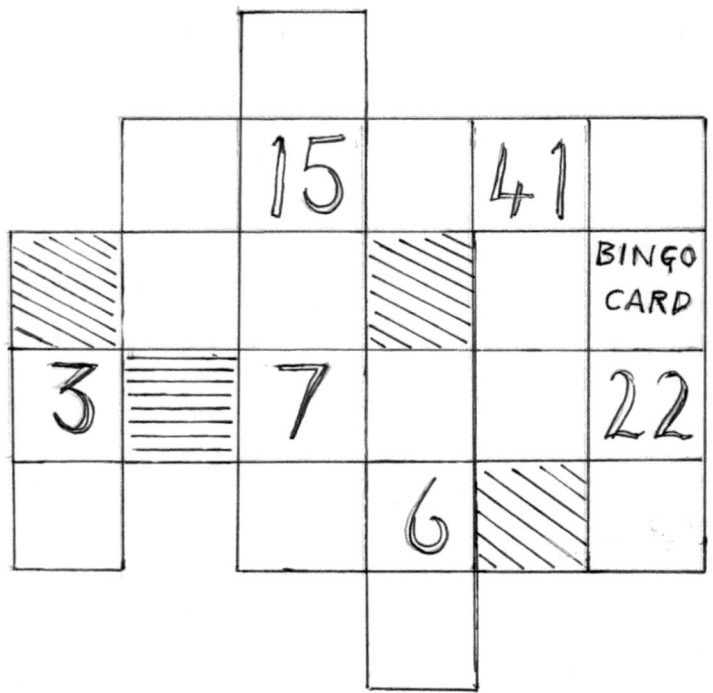

A Bitter Thought.   (July 1967)

Don't you ever again condemn us!
You, who think yourselves so grown up.
You, who hide and criticize.
You who point your money grabbing finger.

You can't complain of younger sets
Who spend extravagantly about the town,
Who, given dainty dress from you
Have changed it to a hideous wardrobe
In their generation.

How can you curb their freedom
For no apparent reason?
Why do you scorn and act derisively?
So unnecessarily,
Such a waste of time.

But you who are used to wasting time
In Bingo Halls[iii]
And twisting one-armed bandits
Should be a little humbler.

Do we youngsters point accusingly at you?
Or dictate how you should spend your time?
No —— we don't;
But now I will.

(cont'd)

Live your last days with your family
Don't neglect a husband, wife or pink fat baby,
It makes us wonder:
Don't you love them?
Don't you need them?
Why not spend your one life with them?

You nod your mechanically minded head.
You say you do,
You say you do.
But why then leave them every day
To buy a bingo book
With money really meant for food.
To spend the rent and satisfy
Your selfish needs.
Do you know, you really are
More childlike than a child?

And there you are
Fumbling for excuses.
Justifying your rights,
Trying to ease your conscience –
Or do I over estimate you there?
Perhaps you do not have a conscience.

You, who cry to us
"It is only a minority who squander
What was originally intended
To house keep.
Besides the teenage kids
Extravagantly spend as well."

(cont'd)

But we do not reply it is only
A squandering minority
As is that part of us
Who are accused of vandalism.
We answer simply:
It is you who have more responsibility,
Our time will come.
And when it does
Let us new adult heads
Spare our children
From jealous abuse, because we shall be old,
And they shall be young.
And let us in our old age
Deserve more respect

For living admirably.

SNOW (1963)[iv]

Glistening, gleaming,
Snowy bright,
Soft and silvery,
Pure and white,
Snowing, snowing
Hard and glowing,
Crispy lumps,
Flakes are flowing.
Stiff and frozen,
Falling, falling,
Thicker, thicker,
Growing, growing.
Silver soft,
Thick and fast,
However longer
Will snow last?
Cruel and freezing,
Biting cold,
Beauty slender,
Gleaming glowing,
Bright and firm
Snowing, snowing.

(cont'd)

Fast and flowing
Comes the snow,
Stays the snow,
Icy cold;
Crispy white,
Brave and bold,
In the night
Frozen hard;
Here to stay,
Melted by sun,
Goes away.

A Poem of Occasion.   (Oct. 1967)

The midnight hour sounds.
As one old day dies down,
Another springs up fresh and new
As that old day once was.

The silent song of dawning day
Will see the flower op' her eye;
Will see the sun through transparent mists
Climb up that wall of blue.

And then the trees awake.

Slowly, feint and far afield
The children, pattering nimble feet
And raising arms in ecstasy,
Praising all the land.

And green hills stand, purple in the mist.

Part II.

They rake it in, the yellow corn,
That whirling wheat, that whirling wheat.
They store it up, the yellow corn,
For us to eat, for us to eat.

That prosperous part of all the year
That summer sends to put us right.
When hungry bellies want and wail,
But still they want and wail.

I want to touch his yellow hair
So soft:
Yet do I dare?
I'd like to gaze into his eyes
So blue:
Yet this I could not do.
Reflections I could surely see
Might make me hide my eyes from me.

His fingers folding into mine
Feel so fine:
His loving look I took
And then returned.
So why does all the morning dew
Seem like teardrops in disguise?

Hasty Youth.   (Nov. 1967)

Though I be forty-five and fat,
I feel like twenty-four, no more than that.
My youth has slipped away from me
And prettier days I will not see.
These legs that creep and crawl around
No longer jitterbug the ground.
My teeth are gone, and sight as well,
But never mind; oh what the hell.
Nuts I suck instead of chew,
The sights the soar eyes only view.
So who am I to dare complain?
I'm quite content to cease my reign
Of maidenhead, long past and gone.
These grey hairs helped to speed it on.

Flowery Thoughts.   (Nov. 1967)

Flower-power's the 'in thing'
To be a sunshine hippy king
Or Queen with rosemary in her hair,
And live a life without a care.
But look you rebels with a cause,
This is no way to show your strife.
Though you say you go in peace
And symbolize the love in life,
Your aim subconsciously it seems
Goes far beyond these flowery schemes.
Youth understands you want to erase
Dead society's falsely-face.
Your target's lost by youth's confusion,
Shattered bewilderment, disillusion.

PRIDE.   (Nov. 1967)

The price of pride is far too great,
I know for I did contemplate
The pros and cons and do discover
Disadvantages outweigh the other.
The seventh sin of manly vice
Is thought by some as being nice,
But this my friend is far from true,
I say it with conviction too.
Persons plagued with such disease
Are always snobs and ill at ease.
They suffer from what neighbours say
And feel that pride will cleanse their way.
These poor fools themselves have cursed,
Of all sins, pride is the worst.

A Pessimistic View, or Cynicism.   (Jan. 1968)

Do you really think they give a damn?
And do you really think they care for you
Or think of you from time to time?
Oh no my friend, but friend is such a mean word;
Oh no dear chum, you are misled.
They would just as sooner you were dead,
Or on the way, at least.

You can't surely mean that.
That you believe and trust those people.
Those people who belittle you, and ridicule
And say what they don't mean,
And don't say what they do mean,
But mean is such a meaningless word.
And you have far to go in making meaners out.

If only there were some
Who mean and say in one breath.
You think there are? Yes, so do I.
Don't be surprised that I should think so too.
I mean to say,
There must be some sincerity lingering on.

I don't mean to crush your world,
Your world of would be make believe.
Wherein if you could 'see the puppets dallying'ᵛ
You would think again.

I want to show you things that are,
But first you must know the things that are
Are the things that are not.
It is merely a matter of defacing face value
To find the face that is there.

1968 Babe.

She had red hair,
She had green eyes;
And one of those looks that could hypnotize.

She had soft hair,
She had large eyes;
And a shape that was sure to tantalize.

With her slinky body
And her headful of hair
Dangling down like she hadn't a care.

She could be real charming
She could be real rude;
"She could really getcha going if she was in the mood,"

Her curves were many
And her curves were alright;
Supple and smooth for a deb's delight.

A cool polished gay girl
One aim in life will do;
"Make sure you get the world
'Afore the world gets you."

She had one aim
And her aim would be,
"To get everybody loving me! me! me!"

Her name was girl,
Or her name was woman;
"But whatever her name it was always Vanity."

(cont'd)

Vanity Plain Jane
Or Vanity Fair,
Vanity Bitch with a shine in her hair.

Some girls are pretty
Some girls are not,
"You cant give away what you have not got."

She had one face
And her face was false.
"Say, why have marriage if ya have divorce?"

She wore the mini
Up to her waist,
"And wondered why she was never chaste[vi]."

She used the bed
Without shame,
"For her sexed up version of the virgin game."

To indulge in sex
Is a terrible sin,
Our Lord God says you must be a virgin

Like the Virgin Mary
Who had a baby boy.
"How the hell she get to be a virginal mother?"

Elegy: On her plight.

I've known someone,
Ten years he says,
But only known
The face.

I used to like
This someone once,
Before he fell
From grace.

My fondness waned,
No more to find
In him a perfect
Case.

But though I thought
That fondness gone,
My heart had saved
A space.

And if I like him,
As before,
Might my feelings
Be erased?

But if I go
Away again,
I think it would be
Me disgraced,

For I find
I really care
About his mind
And face.

And Barclay's Banks
And football fields
Now don't seem so
Misplaced.

And I hope
He thinks of me
As feminine as silk
And lace.

And I hope
He notices
Some womanly ways
Of grace.

But our thoughts
Have little time
Before they'll be
Defaced,

When I'll go one way,
He another.
So is it all
A waste?

A Casual Decision   (1968)

You can make me happy,
Or sad,
The choice is yours.

And you have chosen.

Mummy, Are You Leaving?

Mummy, mummy, mummy, are you leaving,
Deceiving me, my daddy, and my baby brother?
Mother, please don't go.

You look at us with unsad eyes,
You don't tell lies, you give us up the truth.

Believing you would stay and make us happy
We took you for granted.

Just you look at my daddy, he'll be so lonely,
Only wanting you to stay forever,
Never leave my mummy darling
'Cos we love you so.

To Michael, Michael, and Norman.   (Jan. 1969)

It sickens me
To see
Students apathetic;
Dull, useless,
Lethargic …
Lacking in enthusiasm
And even understanding.

And it sickens me
To see
A poem expressing this.

But more than this
It makes me want to spew
At students who
Can criticize these faults
When they are just the same.

A Hoax to Confuse Your Trail of Determining What's Next

If I were to reveal to you my true feelings
Every time
It would be like turning myself inside out
Like giving you a poetry book which I wrote
Is that what you want
A day to day calendar
Of what the weather will be like
Are you thinking of preparing an umbrella
For when it rains
Or a sunshade and sandals when it's fine
How exciting!
Could keep a journal too of what is going to happen
(What about becoming a fortune-teller?)

How about finding yourself caught in the rain
– No umbrella – wow!
Who cares if it's wet
Why not enjoy it
Hold your head back and open your mouth
Feel the rain pour in
Watch your beautiful hair reflected in a puddle
Become straight and sticky

Watch the drops roll off your nose
Producing images of you
In a single ripple

People seem to have a thing about blocking out
The natural, the realistic,
Prefer to be dusty dirty dry
Hiding under that umbrella

(cont'd)

Well then people –
Rot!

But you baby
I can give you rain for your sunshade
And sunshine for your umbrella

But when that dries up
What then –

Bread for your butter
And fish with your chips?

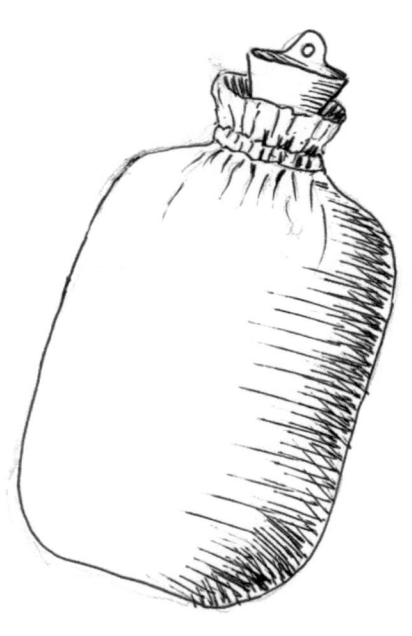

Substitute   (March 1969)

Instead of soft and silky skin
Legs entwining
Instead of warm and special feelings
Arms embracing
Spontaneous kiss
Tender word
Or security

A rubber water bottle

Confessions.   (1967)

Okay, so I'll come clean
Nothing to lose anyway

So I do go in for a little sentimental crap
From time to time.
(Just to keep up appearances you understand.)

Okay, so I get the maternal instinct
See me walking children to school
My kids
Practice taking myself seriously
(Just in case I'll need to.)

Okay, so imagine how I'll look
In brown tweed suits
Cork heel shoes
Spreading rolls of fat and grey wrinkles,
(But I've no imagination.)

It's no good

I can't come
Completely clean
Though all there is to lose
Is face.

Even now you are to be found
In every crevice of my mind.

After December I thought you would leave.
And you did for a while.
But you had to come back
In January, February, March … .
And now it's May.

Baby, you're a long time going.

Obsession makes me cling to things
I haven't got
Perhaps don't want
But think I need,
You bastard

And if I were to say
I still care,
You wouldn't laugh

Would you?

On my own again   (July 1967)

On my own again
That's the only way to be
Finding in people
Something I don't need
Best to say nothing, though
Leaving you
Pink jeans ending
Where long hair takes over
Felt you standing at the door
Looking for a moment.
Even miss the hamster.

On Considering Whether One Should Be So Aloof.[vii]   (1969)

Despite a barrier
Of other people, and being female proud,
Not wanting to stumble
Upon barbed wire too sharp to hold.
I gave you what I could safely say
Was enough.

Within a boundary of restraint,
Fake indifference, and vanity for keeping cool,
You kept silent.
There was little left for even
A weak wall of understanding.

And anyway,
Who could be sure that you approved?
Eyes no longer tell tales
But only half truths,
Saying little
And meaning even less.
So imagination over-rides and you see
What isn't there.

Lest this should happen, you my baby
Will have to be more definite

For all I see is an Afghani waistcoat
Waiting impatiently to be given to a friend.

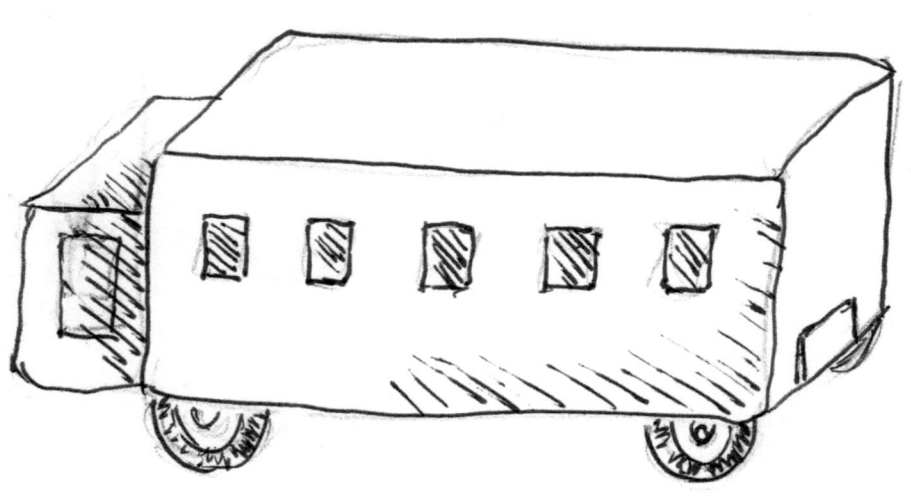

A Crowded Box[viii] (1969 August – Jaipur.)

A crowded box
Leaking sweat
And aggravation
No room for tolerance
After the first six weeks
Of acute politeness
Change to basic
Shapes of one's self.

If ever   (1969. August – Jaipur)

If ever
I again visit a mind like yours
Intruding on my own
Likeness
Then let me know
Before it is too late.

A Silent Look[ix].   (1970)

Only a silent look
Of melancholy eyes
That speak for themselves
In softly tones
Of anguish.

Only a passing thought
Of what a damnable thing
That trust can be.

Only a silent ache
Not one to cause a tear
To trickle down
And tell a tale to all.

Just a lonely song
Of emptiness and longing
While you are there
And I am here
My love.

Tomorrow I Shall Sparkle

Tomorrow I shall sparkle
Today I am dim
Like the candle whose wick's
Running low no reason
To smile await special treats
Nice surprise bouquet of flowers
Sweet tangerines or kisses
Tender feelings have faded
Like old blue jeans or
a water colour bleached by the sun

My face has grown hard
I call it the leather look spent
Cracked dry pursed lips empty
What happened to glistening eyes
Embraces excited chatter outings
Being spoilt just a little
From time to time
Today I am dull dark but tomorrow …

Tomorrow I shall sparkle

Kurzbiografie

Karen Ann Tepperis geb. Lake wird am 11. September 1949 in London geboren, geht dort zur Schule, studiert Anglistik, Theater und Kunst am Rolle College in Exmouth (Devon), spielt Theater, besingt eigene Schallplatten und reist.

Sie kommt 1973 nach Deutschland und verlagert ihren Lebensmittelpunkt nach Darmstadt.

Durch viele erfolgreiche Teilnahmen an Talentwettbewerben verdient sie sich durch ihren Gesang einen Plattenvertrag bei EMI Electrola, wird Gründungsmitglied des Frauentrios „Arabesque", produziert Hits, welche zwei Goldene Schallplatten erhalten.

Zeitgleich studiert sie in Frankfurt an der Johann Wolfgang Goethe-Universität Kunst und Anglistik, schließt mit zwei Staatsexamen ab und wird Lehrerin an einem privaten Darmstädter Gymnasium.

Sie heiratet, hat zwei Söhne … und einen Kater.

Short Biography

Karen Ann Tepperis née Lake is born in London on 11th September, 1949. She goes to school there, studies English, art and drama at Rolle College in Exmouth (Devon), plays in several theatrical plays, records own records and travels.

1973 she comes to Germany and creates the centre of her life in Darmstadt.

Her singing earns her a record contract at EMI Electrola after winning several talent contests. She becomes a member of the girl group "Arabesque", releases records which win two Golden Records.

Simultaneously she studies art and English at the Johann Wolfgang Goethe-University in Frankfurt, finishes with two state examinations and becomes teacher at a private grammar school in Darmstadt.

She gets married, has two sons … and a tomcat.

COMMENTS

[i] Exmouth (Devon)

[ii] Rolle College in Exmouth

[iii] In 1967 the game 'Bingo' was very popular amongst adults in England. There were large halls only used for Bingo, where many of the working classes spent a lot of their time, and money. (Gambling - a drug?)

[iv] winner of the county's poetry contest in London, 1963

[v] from Shakespeare's Hamlet

[vi] play on words: 'chased' and 'chaste'

[vii] 20th August, 1969, travelling in Oxford coach to La Hore, Pakistan.

[viii] Depiction of Comex Coach. 1969 journey to India.

[ix] After leaving India and a friend.

www.the-pink-puff.de